ON PURPOSE

ON PURPOSE

LESSONS IN LIFE AND HEALTH FROM
THE FROG, THE DUNG BEETLE, AND JULIA

Written by

Victor J. Strecher

Illustrated by

Kody Chamberlain

DUNG
BEETLE
PRESS

Published in the United States of America by Dung Beetle Press, Ann Arbor, Michigan

Manufactured in Michigan, United States of America

First Edition

Library of Congress Cataloging-in-Publication Data

Strecher, Victor.

On Purpose: Lessons in Life and Health from the Frog, the Dung Beetle, and Julia / written by Victor J. Strecher; illustrated by Kody Chamberlain. – 1st ed.

ISBN 9781940594002

1. Purpose in life 2. Philosophy 3. Death 4. Behavior change 5. Health

Library of Congress Control Number: 2013948842

Illustrations by Kody Chamberlain

Lettering by Kel Nuttall

Visit us at www.dungbeetlepress.org

For you, Julia.

Please remember me, fondly

I heard from someone you're still pretty

And then they went on to say that the Pearly Gates

Had some eloquent graffiti

– Iron & Wine

Transformations: Foreword to *On Purpose*

A friend of mine called me recently to let me know he was running late.

"So much traffic, what a nightmare!" he exclaimed.

"No, that's not a nightmare," I replied. "That's an inconvenience."

Jonas Salk, who discovered the polio vaccine, shared with me just before he died, "I have had dreams and I have had nightmares. I overcame my nightmares because of my dreams."

So did Vic Strecher. Losing a child is a nightmare. And in this extraordinary book, he invites us to go on a voyage of discovery with him: a transformational journey of nightmares into golden dreams; unimaginable suffering into profound joy; and nihilism into deep meaning.

I first met Vic at the 2009 TEDMED conference in San Diego, California. His pioneering research on interactive media for promoting health and preventing disease really wowed the audience—and me. We both understood that the root cause of so many chronic diseases (which account for about 75% of America's $2.8 trillion in healthcare costs) is the lifestyle choices that we make. His work has helped change the health behaviors of millions of people.

When Vic's daughter, Julia, was only seven months old, he and his wife, Jeri, were told that Julia had only a month to live. She had a heart transplant and lived, but it was a difficult life. At the age of nine, she almost died and needed a second heart transplant. Although she did well for a while, when she was only 19, she suddenly died.

Out of this incomprehensible suffering has come this beautiful book. It shows the importance of finding a transcendent purpose that is larger than ourselves.

If it's meaningful, it's sustainable.
If it's meaningful, it's bearable.
As the philosopher Nietzche wrote, "He who has a *why* to live for can bear almost any *how*."

Our suffering—even the unfathomable loss of a beloved daughter—can be a catalyst for spiritual transformation, or it can overwhelm us. While we can't always change what happens to us, we can influence how we experience what happens. We have more choice than we may realize.

This is true for everyday actions as well. When we choose not to do things that we otherwise could do, it imbues the choices we do make with deep meaning and purpose.

"I feel deprived because I can't eat this type of food" leads to struggle and deprivation and is not sustainable.

"I'm choosing not to eat this food because I feel so much better, what I gain is so much more than what I give up" is sustainable. So is, "I want to live longer so I can have more time to do things that are meaningful to me."

Dr. Elizabeth Blackburn was awarded the Nobel Prize in Medicine in 2009 for discovering telomerase, an enzyme that repairs and lengthens our telomeres, the ends of our chromosomes that control aging. As our telomeres get shorter, our lives get shorter.

She and her colleagues at UCSF, including Dr. Elissa Epel, found that women who were under chronic emotional stress (because they were caregivers of parents with Alzheimer's disease or children with autism) had shorter telomeres. The more stressed they felt, and the longer they felt that way, the shorter their telomeres. It was the first study showing that there is a genetic basis explaining why chronic emotional stress may shorten your life.

What I found even more interesting was that the most important determinant of how chronic emotional stress affected these women's telomeres was their *perception* of stress. If you *feel* stressed, you *are* stressed. Two women might be in similar life situations, but one was coping with it much better than another using many of the precepts outlined in this book—meditation, community, service, and so on—to find inner meaning and peace. Even if a woman was under challenging life situations, if she coped with it well and didn't experience it as stressful, her telomeres were not as affected.

Fortunately, it works both ways, for better and for worse. Dr. Blackburn, our colleagues and I recently published the first controlled study showing that comprehensive lifestyle changes that incorporate the ideas in this book significantly increase telomere length. Even on a genetic and chromosomal level, our perceptions of meaning influence our survival.

Decades earlier, in his classic book, "*Man's Search for Meaning*," Viktor Frankl made a similar observation. Even in the extreme stress of a concentration camp in Nazi Germany, two inmates in the same camp with similar life situations had very different outcomes. One survived, one did not. He found that those inmates who were able to find meaning even in this dire situation were much more likely to survive. "I want to live to see my child grow up. I want to dance at their wedding." And so on.

Meaning is malleable. You can take it out, and you can put it in.

It's a lot more fun to put meaning in your life than to take it out.

I first learned this when I was in my first year of college. I was able to take all the meaning out of everything, devolving into a downward spiral of nihilism and depression, and it almost killed me.

Since then, I've been learning how to put meaning back into everything by making it sacred.

We are always making choices, sacrifices. The word "sacrifice" has an austere, depriving connotation to it. But people don't usually think about that when they put money aside for their kids going to college, or a wedding. These choices—what we choose not to do as well as what to do—bring meaning into our lives.

In this context, choosing to eat and live differently can be a joyful spiritual practice rather than one leaving you feeling deprived or depressed. We can enjoy life more fully by making these conscious choices.

Instead of resolving to make changes in diet and lifestyle out of a sense of austerity, deprivation, and asceticism, I find it to be much more effective—and fun—to be motivated by feelings of love, joy, and ecstasy.

When we consciously choose not to do things that we otherwise could do, it makes them sacred. When I was a teenager, I thought "sacred" meant "boring"—something dry and old, gathering mold and dust. Definitely *not* fun.

Now, I understand that "sacred" is just another way of describing what is the most special and therefore the *most* meaningful, the *most* intimate, the *most* erotic, the *most* exciting, the *most* powerful, the *most* ecstatic, the *most* joyful, the *most* playful.

The most fun.

If what you gain is more than what you give up, then it's sustainable. Abundance is sustainable; deprivation is not. Joy is sustainable; repression and fear are not. "It's good for me" is not sustainable; "it's fun for me" is. Fear of dying is not sustainable; joy of living is.

Sometimes, I forget what I know. When I do, I often suffer, and the suffering reminds me. In this context, it becomes my teacher rather than my punishment, re-minding me.

That's what the most enlightened spiritual teachers have taught through the millennia: how to live a joyful life, right here and now. Ways of living in the world that make it a lot more fun and juicy and happy.

Not for some future rewards—going to heaven, getting a gold star, an award, or good karma. Rather, these are approaches to living that bring happiness and help us avoid suffering, in this very moment. "My religion is happiness," said the Dalai Lama.

Writing this book has given Vic Strecher a powerful sense of meaning. Reading it may do the same for you. It did for me. The light drives out the darkness, and we can experience our world anew, filled with pleasure, joy, and meaning.

Dean Ornish, M.D.
Founder and President,
Preventive Medicine Research Institute
Clinical Professor of Medicine,
University of California, San Francisco
author, *The Spectrum*
www.ornish.com

CONTENTS

Prologue:
A DREAM

The breeze at dawn has secrets to
tell you. Don't go back to sleep.

You must ask for what you really
want. Don't go back to sleep.

People are going back and forth across the
doorsill where the two worlds touch.

The door is round and open.
Don't go back to sleep.

Mewlana Jalaluddin Rumi [13th Century]

silence: just now an angel crossed,
huge as the life of a hundred suns

Octavio Paz

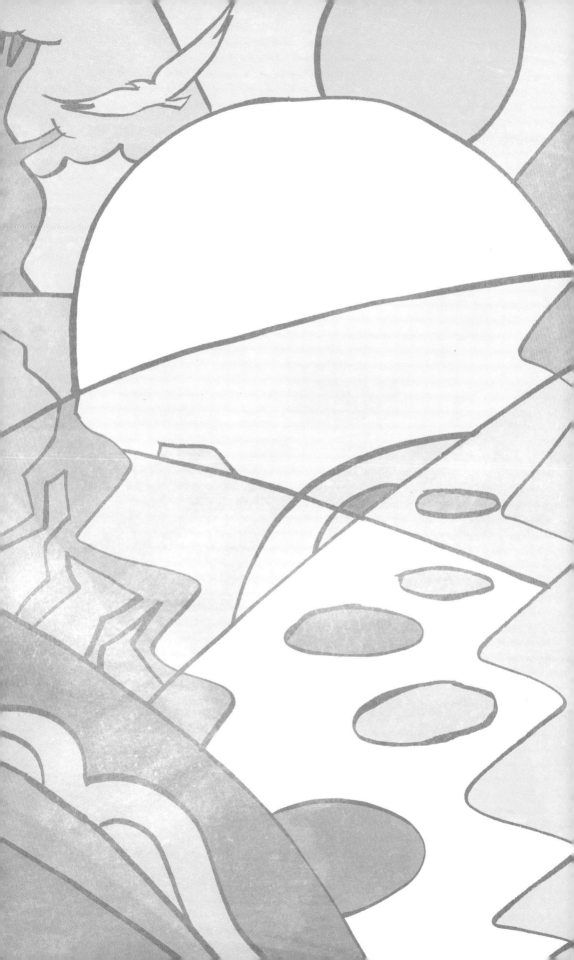

7

AS THE SUN WAS COMING UP, SOMETHING HAPPENED. A MOMENT OF UNITY WITH THE SUN AND THE WATER...AND WITH JULIA. TELLING ME THAT I NEEDED TO MOVE FORWARD.

THEN I REALIZED THAT IT WAS FATHER'S DAY, JUNE 20, 2010. THIS WAS HER GIFT TO ME.

Lesson 1

DEATH OR LIFE?

I felt that what I was standing
on had given way, that I had no
foundation to stand on, that that
which I lived by no longer existed,
and that I had nothing to live by.

Leo Tolstoy

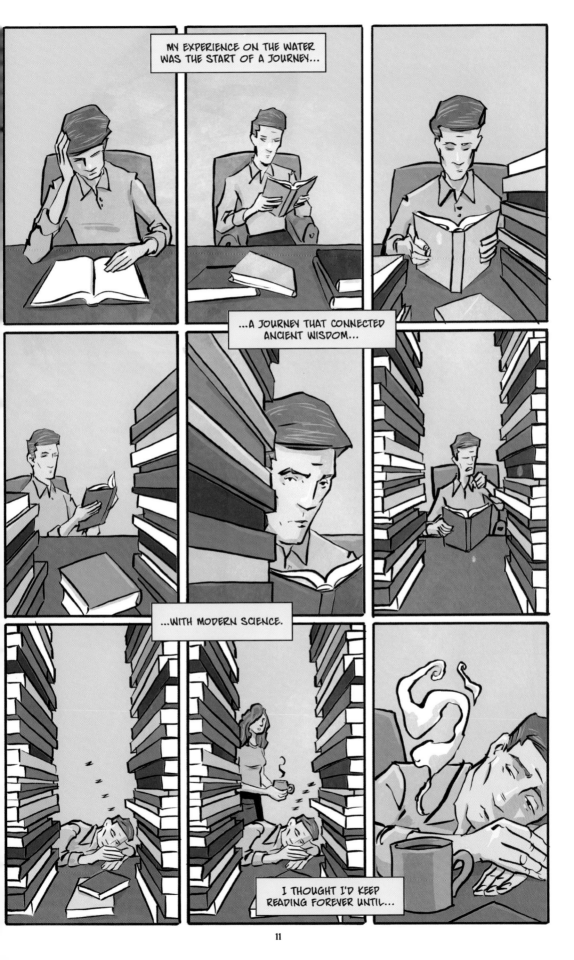

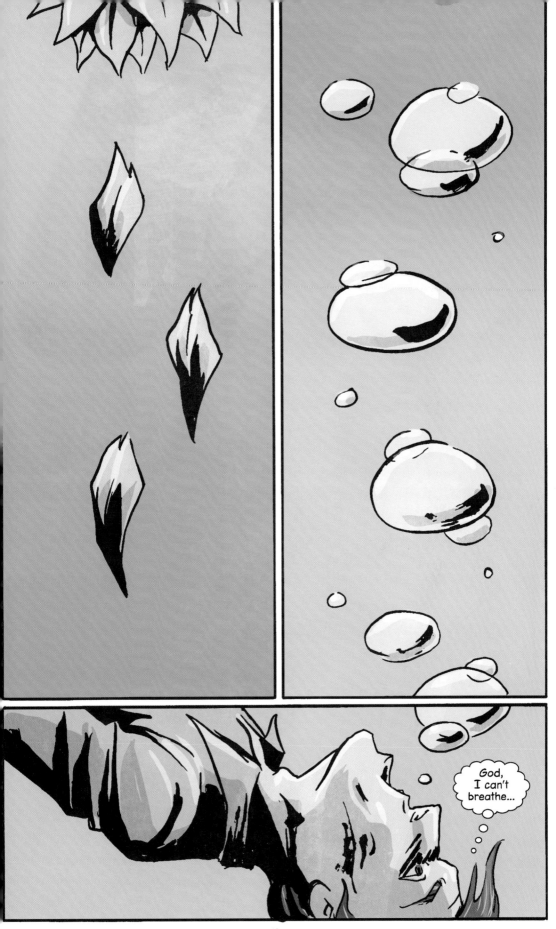

God,
I can't
breathe...

Lesson 2

DEFENSIVENESS

Everyone of us is shadowed by
an illusory person: a false self.

Thomas Merton

All in all it's just another
brick in the wall.

Pink Floyd

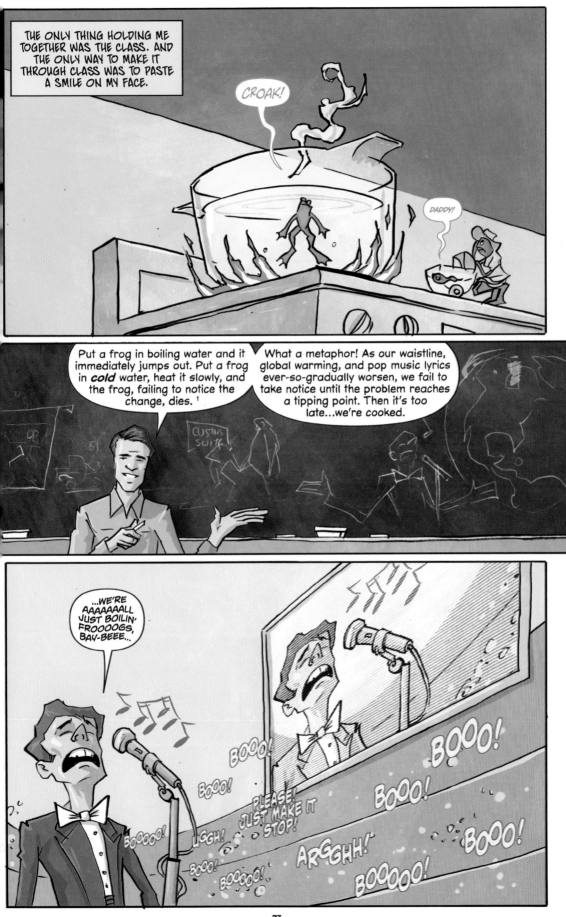

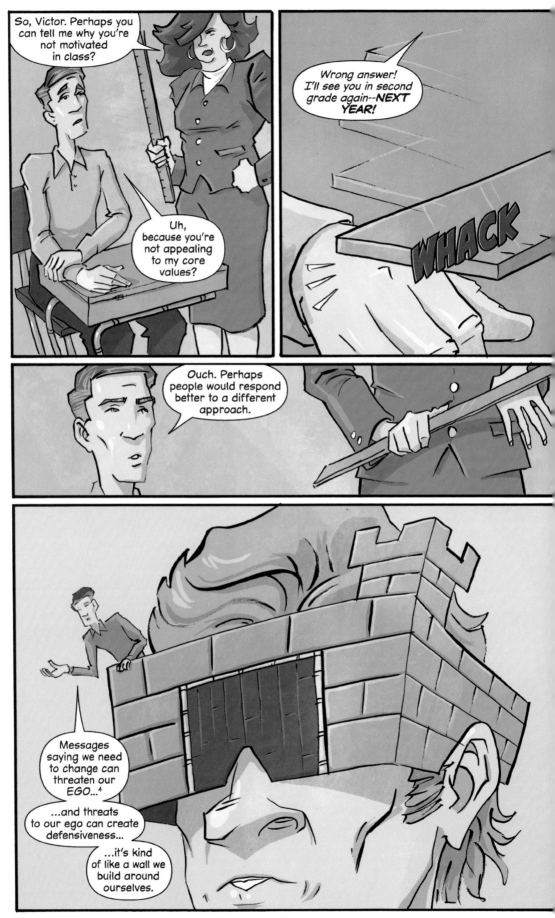

30

33

34

RACHEL MADDOW

BILL O'REILLY

INSTEAD OF SELECTING INFORMATION SOURCES THAT ONLY REINFORCE OUR SELVES, WE MIGHT BECOME LESS DEFENSIVE BY OPENING THE DRAWBRIDGE, EVERY ONCE IN A WHILE, TO PEOPLE WHO DON'T. YOU DON'T HAVE TO AGREE WITH THEM BUT YOU MIGHT BENEFIT FROM A DEEPER UNDERSTANDING OF THEIR PERSPECTIVES. 7

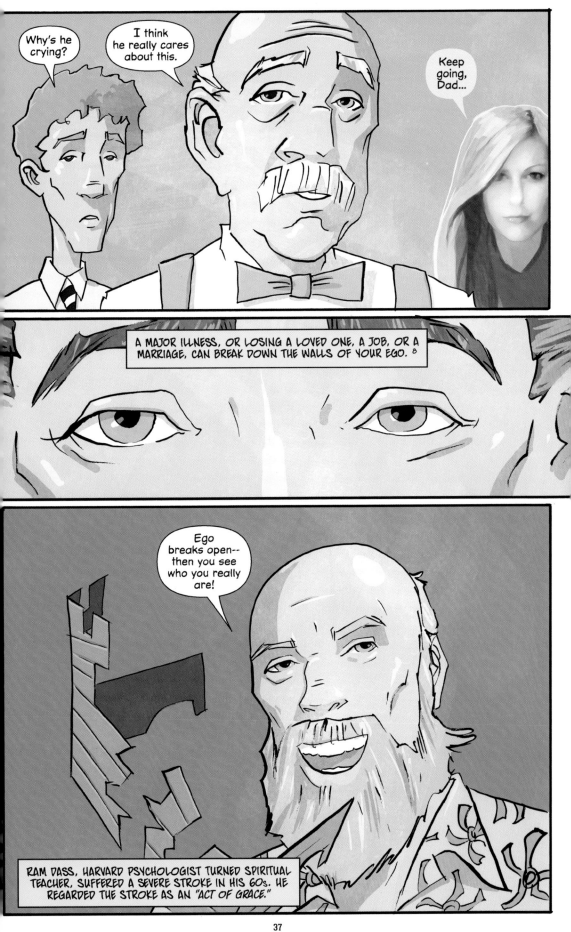

42

43

Lesson 3

SELF-TRANSCENDENCE

Only to the extent that someone is living out this self-transcendence of human existence, is he truly human or does he become his true self. He becomes so, not by concerning himself with his self's actualization, but by forgetting himself and giving himself, overlooking himself and focusing outward.

Viktor Frankl

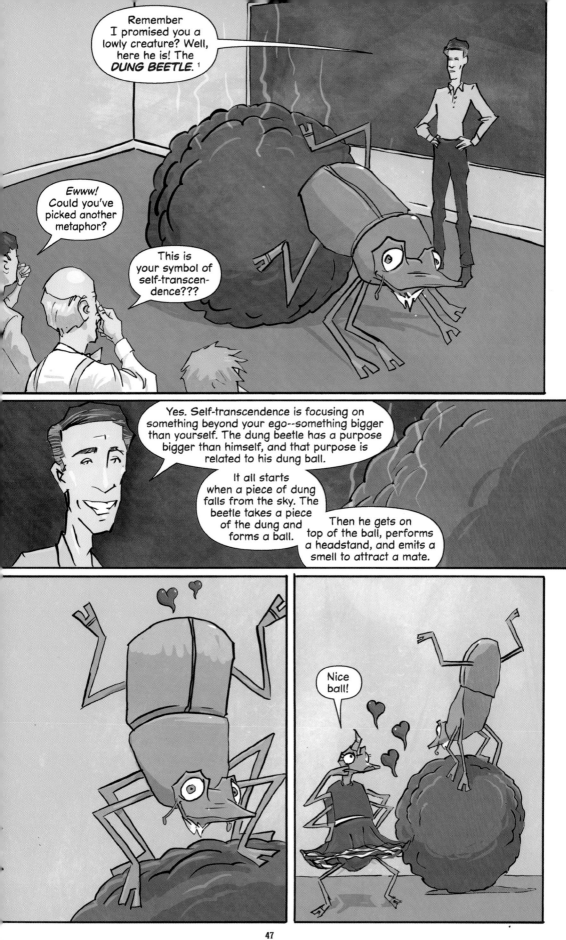

THE DUNG BEETLES ROLL THEIR BALL IN A STRAIGHT LINE TOWARD A DESTINATION, DESPITE TERRAIN, WEATHER, THIEVES, OR ANY OTHER OBSTACLE.

IF YOU SEARCHED THE ENTIRE WORLD OF LIVING ORGANISMS--FROM BACTERIA TO PRESIDENTS--YOU'D BE HARD-PRESSED TO FIND ONE THAT LIVES ITS LIFE WITH SUCH A STRONG PURPOSE. *THIS IS A BUG ON A MISSION.* [2]

THE EGYPTIAN SCARAB WAS KHEPRI, THE GOD WHOSE NAME MEANS "TO COME INTO BEING." KHEPRI WAS RESPONSIBLE FOR ROLLING THE SUN UP OVER THE HORIZON EVERY MORNING AND SYMBOLIZED REBIRTH AND TRANSFORMATION. [3]

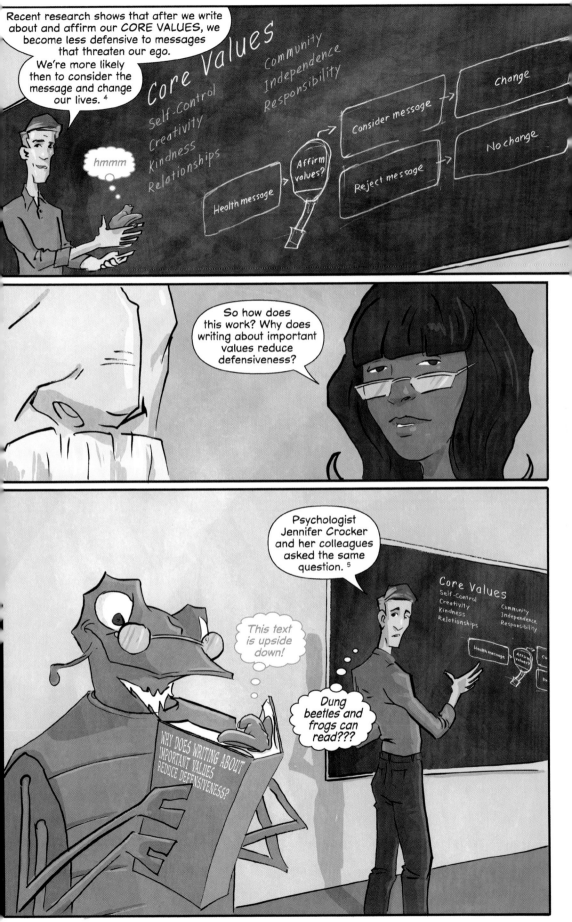

In fact, two highly-respected scientists, Chris Peterson and Martin Seligman, wrote that "Transcendence can be something or someone earthly that inspires awe, hope, or even gratitude--anything that makes our everyday concerns seem trifling and the self seem small." [6]

Let's look at how a few others considered the concept of "self-transcendence."

Writing over 60 years ago about "man's deep-seated urge to self-transcendence," Aldous Huxley considered three directions we can take:

Ascending self-transcendence was purely spiritual. Huxley practiced a Hindu philosophy, and believed that very few people would achieve ascending transcendence to *nirvana* through *moksha*, or liberation from the ego.

But Huxley knew that other people attempt to escape their ego through *descending* transcendence, primarily alcohol and drugs.

I experimented with descending transcendence myself... [7]

What matters is the awareness, if only for an hour or two, if only for a few minutes, of being someone or, more often something other than the insulated self.

Wow.

You've heard of Maslow's Hierarchy? For most of his career, Abraham Maslow, the founder of Humanistic Psychology, viewed SELF-ACTUALIZATION as the pinnacle of human existence--the ultimate stage after other more basic needs have been met.
Self-actualizers, whether they're custodians or astronauts, have a deep desire to reach their full potential in life.
But later in his life, Maslow found special qualities in people who had a purpose reaching beyond their own interests.
"That's one small step for man, one giant leap for mankind..."
SELF-ACTUALIZATION
ESTEEM NEEDS
SOCIAL NEEDS
SAFETY NEEDS
PHYSIOLOGICAL NEEDS

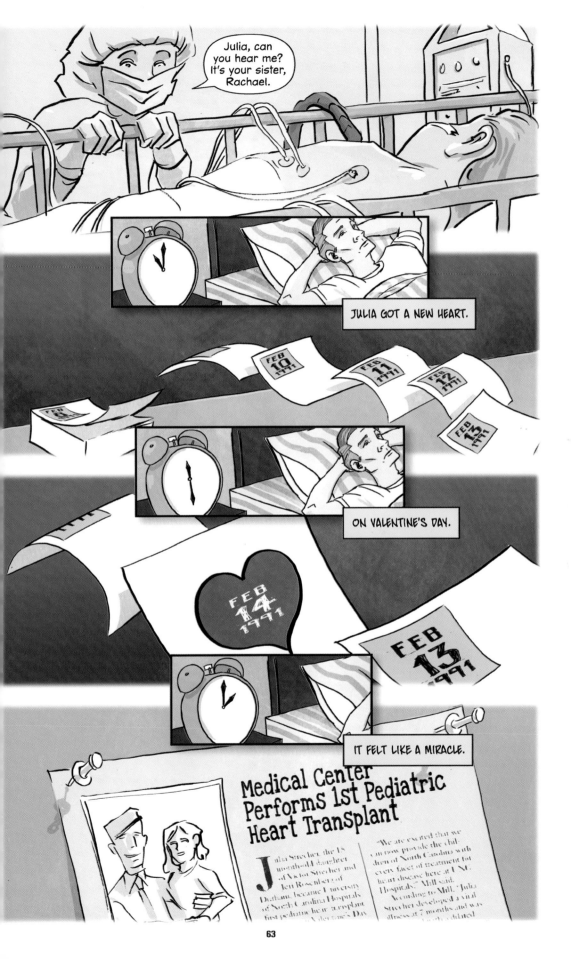

Lesson 4

PURPOSE

Every life needs a purpose to which
it can give the energies of its mind and
the enthusiasm of its heart.

Saint Francis of Assisi [12th Century]

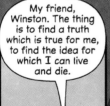

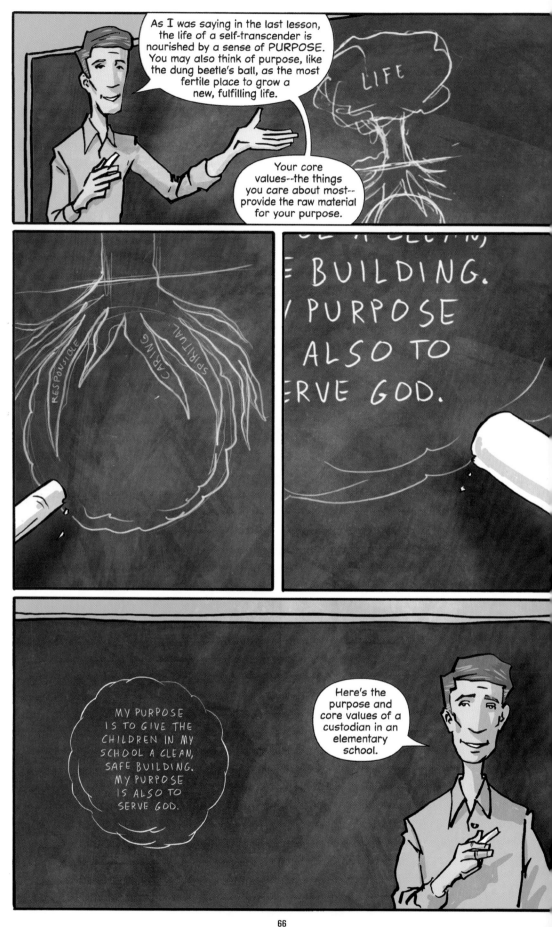

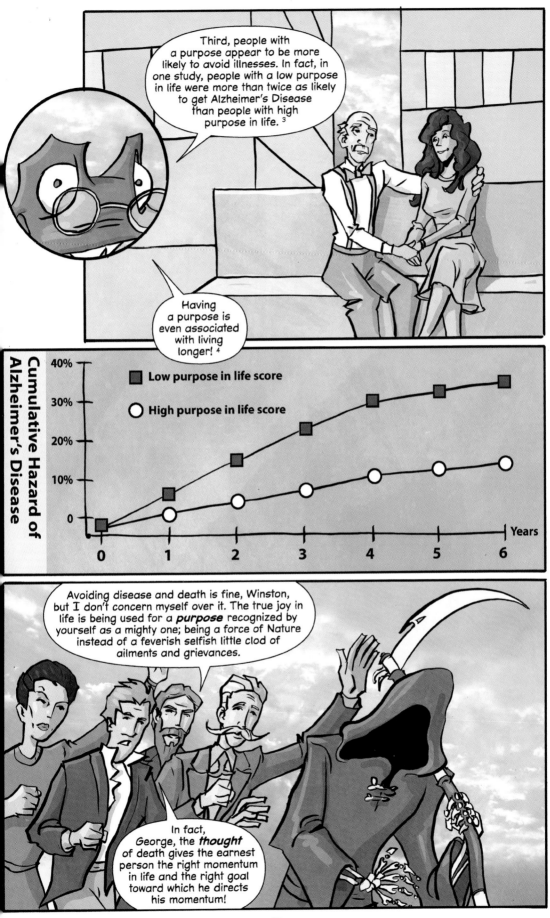

Third, people with a purpose appear to be more likely to avoid illnesses. In fact, in one study, people with a low purpose in life were more than twice as likely to get Alzheimer's Disease than people with high purpose in life. [3]

Having a purpose is even associated with living longer! [4]

Cumulative Hazard of Alzheimer's Disease

■ Low purpose in life score

○ High purpose in life score

40%

30%

20%

10%

0

0   1   2   3   4   5   6   Years

Avoiding disease and death is fine, Winston, but I don't concern myself over it. The true joy in life is being used for a *purpose* recognized by yourself as a mighty one; being a force of Nature instead of a feverish selfish little clod of ailments and grievances.

In fact, George, the *thought* of death gives the earnest person the right momentum in life and the right goal toward which he directs his momentum!

In 2011, Dr. Blackburn was part of a research team that found that meditation increased purpose in life, which in turn *increased telomerase activity!*

They found that "Meditation and other contemplative practices...promote a sense of purpose and direction in life...more genuine contentment and a greater sense of contributing to human welfare."

In other words, having a transcendent purpose can actually *protect your genes!* [5]

PURPOSE

HEALTHY CHROMOSOME

But Western society appears to lack transcendent purpose. We don't seem to be interested in "contributing to human welfare."

We seem to be more focused on making money and becoming famous...

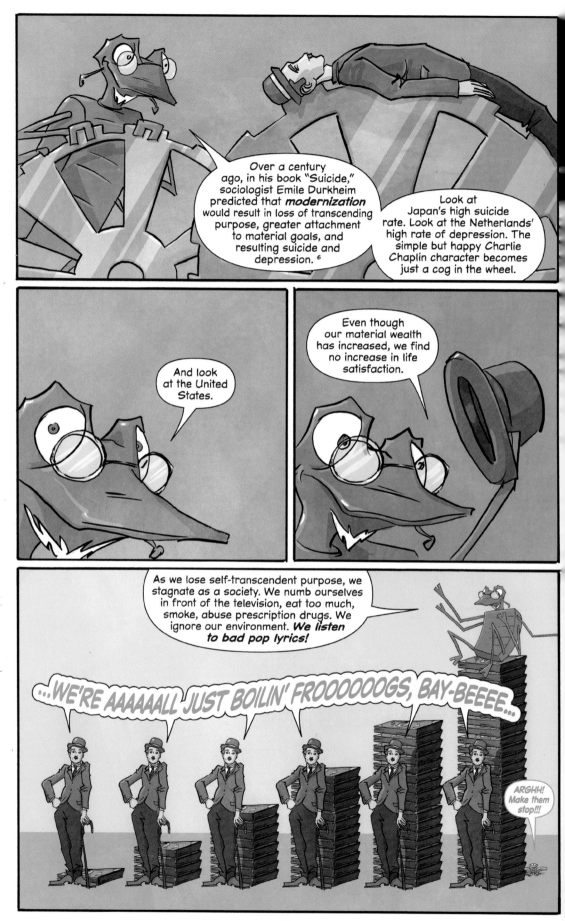

Winston, I'm in the Business School. I'm here to learn how to **make money**. To achieve. To be admired. What's wrong with that? Can't **THESE** values be a part of my purpose?

I was waiting for that question... remember, I'm a dung beetle, not a moralist.

BUT, research shows that self-transcending values are more likely to create well-being and greater willpower to change behavior than what we might call "self-enhancing values."

Self-Transcending: empathy, compassion, being supportive of the needs of others, creating or contributing to something larger than oneself, truth, openness, personal growth, being in mutually supportive and caring relationships

In one study of graduating college students, researchers found that graduates who placed importance upon close relationships, community involvement, and personal growth were, two years later, more likely to have achieved these goals **AND** to have greater **WELL-BEING**, whereas...

...Graduates who aspired more to money, fame, and appearance were, two years later, more likely to have achieved these goals **BUT** had greater **ILL-BEING**. [7]

Self-Enhancing: power, status, wealth, possessions, physical attractiveness, popularity, admiration, prestige

I'm not here to tell you what to believe in, Nick, but I'd suggest choosing your purpose wisely.

BACK AT HOME...

This is amazing. Seneca wrote about the fleeting nature of our lives 2,000 years ago! [8]

SENECA — Consolation to Marcia

'But he died too soon, and before his time.' Imagine in the first place that he had survived -- assign to him as many years in a long life that a man may have: how many, after all, do they comprise? Brought into the world for the briefest of spans, and destined shortly to give up our place to the next person who comes... You may quote me the names of men who had long lives, whose old age has passed into memory, you may count up a hundred and ten years for each of them: when you turn to the contemplation of eternity, that distinction between the shortest and longest of lives will count for nothing, if, having examined the number of years a man has lived, you compare these with the number he has not lived.

His friend Marcia had lost her teenage son three years before and her grief was worst than ever. Seneca wrote her this letter to console her.

I wonder if she was consoled.

I wonder if she drank bourbon?

Consolation to Marcia
by
Lucius Annaeus Seneca

76

Lesson 5

DEATH

If all of us would make an all-out
effort to contemplate our own death,
to deal with our anxieties surrounding
the concept of our death, and to help
others familiarize themselves with these
thoughts, perhaps there could be less
destructiveness around us.

Elizabeth Kubler-Ross

Don't fear the reaper.

Blue Öyster Cult

Ah, yes, the common refrain of man: "I only wish I had done it sooner." I've heard it for ages.

The great poet Lucretius[1] wrote: "So who are you to balk and whine at death? You're almost dead in life, although you walk and breathe. You fritter away most of your time asleep...

...You snore with your eyes open; you never leave off dreaming, and a score of empty nightmares fills your mind and shakes it to the core. Often, addled and dizzy, you don't even know what's wrong."

Well put, Winston! If you lived ten thousand years, why would you care about your dung ball? You'd never roll it to its proper site...never bury it. You'd lose commitment to your purpose. [5]

The Roman Emperor Marcus Aurelius said to *"not act as if you were going to live ten thousand years. Death hangs over you. While you live, while it is in your power, be good."*

Well I believe "being good" is a way to praise and honor *God*. God gives my life meaning and purpose!

When Friedrich Nietzsche shocked the world by stating *"God is dead,"* he was really saying that a traditional role of religion--providing meaning and purpose in people's lives--was waning.

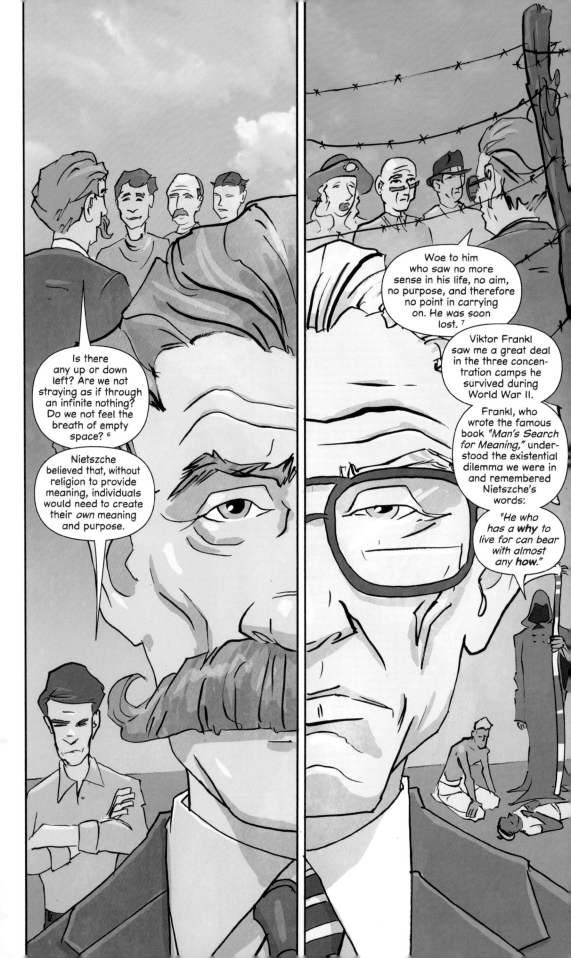

We also see this behavior in infants, before such values can be consciously learned. Research on babies as young as 14 months finds naturally occurring altruistic behavior--babies helping each other fetch out-of-reach objects or opening cabinets. [12]

They do this without any rewards from adults. In fact, external rewards from adults actually undermine the behavior!

CHOCOLATE CHIPS

But Winston, why would evolution select for empathic or altruistic behaviors?

JULIA HAD A DIFFICULT LIFE. AT THE AGE OF NINE SHE ALMOST DIED AND NEEDED A SECOND HEART TRANSPLANT. HER IMMUNE SYSTEM WAS SUPPRESSED AND SHE WAS SICK A LOT. SHE OFTEN DIDN'T HAVE THE ENERGY TO KEEP UP...

...BUT SHE DID KEEP UP. SHE WAS A GIRL SCOUT, WAS ON A SOFTBALL TEAM, SHE HAD GREAT TEACHERS. SHE LOVED TO READ...

...SHE TRAVELED AROUND THE WORLD, WENT TO PROM, HAD GREAT FRIENDS, AND STARTED NURSING SCHOOL...

...EVERY MILESTONE OF HER LIFE FILLED MY HEART WITH JOY AND GRATITUDE. HER STRENGTH TO LIVE A FULFILLING LIFE INSPIRED ME AND GAVE ME STRENGTH...

Lesson 6

CHANGE

To change your life: start immediately;
do it flamboyantly; no exceptions.

William James

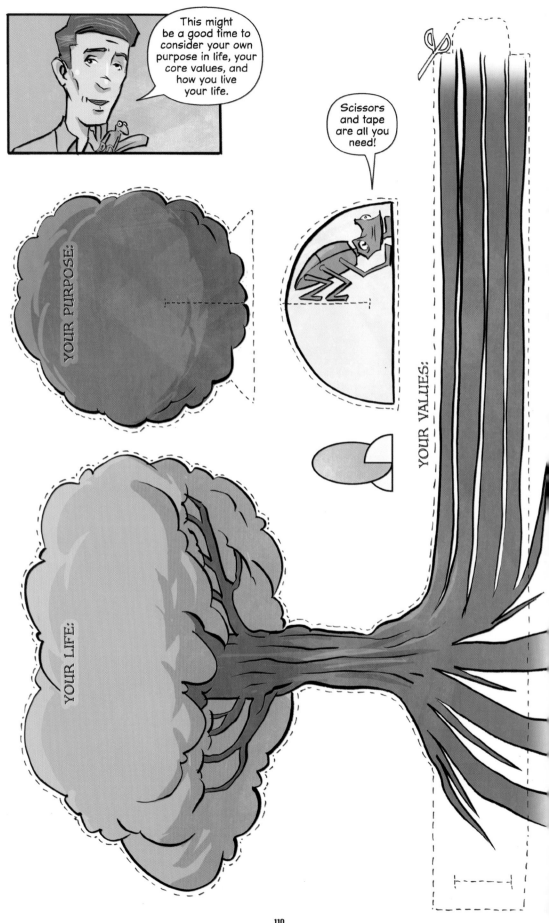

In Lesson 1 I talked about the work of my friend, Dr. Dean Ornish. [4]

He's a master healer...

Thanks, Winston. We've found that changes in lifestyle-- what we eat, how we respond to stress, whether we smoke, how much we exercise--can treat, and actually prevent, heart disease, prostate cancer and Type 2 diabetes.

These changes can increase the expression of positive genes and decrease the expression of genes that make you sick. So we really *can* change our genes!

We've been talking in our class about the importance of having a transcending purpose.

Purpose and meaning are so connected to our work...to our ability to love, to show compassion, and to deepen our relationships with others...to our very survival.

Where's your tree, Vic?

It's not pretty...

I'd like to see it.

Uh...if you don't mind I'd like to finish up early. See you next week, okay?

Lesson 7

LIFE OR DEATH?

Never was space milder, never shared
itself so, nor was nearer. Thousands
of years upon these beetles, deep where
none can use or hinder it, space waits...

Rainer Maria Rilke, from The Scarab

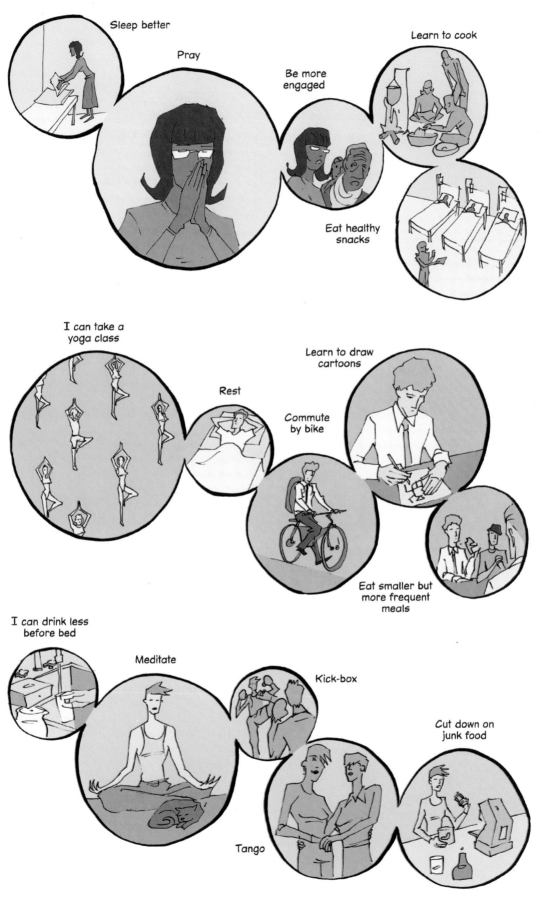

Sleep better

Pray

Be more engaged

Learn to cook

Eat healthy snacks

I can take a yoga class

Rest

Learn to draw cartoons

Commute by bike

Eat smaller but more frequent meals

I can drink less before bed

Meditate

Kick-box

Cut down on junk food

Tango

Epilogue:
A DREAM

Into the ancient pond
A frog jumps
Water's sound!

Basho [16th Century]

131

Are you ready?
Yes, I think so.
Nice jump, Dad!
Did I have a choice?
Of course. You did it on purpose!

But what a shining animal is man,

Who knows, when pain subsides, that is not that,

For worse than that must follow--yet can write

Music; can laugh; play tennis; even plan.

— **Edna St. Vincent Millay**

NOTES

Lesson 1: Death or Life?

1. "What is health?" and "Who gets to define health?" are reasonable, not just academic, questions. The World Health Organization defines health as "a state of complete physical, mental, and social well-being and not merely the absence of disease or infirmity." Do our expenditures for health research and health care reflect this definition?

    In our society, many of the health professionals who determine how our health research and health care expenditures are allocated seem to define health as a "lack of disease and death." In a way, a quantity rather than a quality of life. Not life satisfaction. Not resilience to life's challenges. Not even an ability to function physically, socially, and psychologically in our environment. Some health professionals would categorize these outcomes under the term "mental health." This is a tidy way of removing from the agenda what I consider a truer definition of health. Psychologists, psychiatrists, and social workers deal with mental health. As many physicians will say privately, "real medicine" deals with "physical" diseases. Unfortunately, we in the health field pay little attention to the sciences that focus on what health really is.

2. Japan has had the highest life expectancy for the past decade.

    -   Murray CJL. "Why is Japanese Life Expectancy So High?" *The Lancet* 2011; 378(9797): 1124-1125.

3. Costa Rica has been ranked the "happiest" country in the world in two recent studies of the Happy Planet Index.

    -   "The Happy Planet Index: 2012 Report." *Happy Planet Index*. NEF, 2012.

4. Three researchers from Japan, Daien Oshita, Koji Hattori, and Miho Iwakuma, recently stated, "Although Japan has made amazing technological advances and life expectancy rates are 83 (79 years for men; 86 years for women), more than three million Japanese people commit suicide every year (with some victims younger than 20 years of age)." In 2007, Japan ranked first among females and second among males in suicide rates among all G8 countries. In 2006, Japan had the ninth-highest suicide rate in the world.

    -   Oshita D, Hattori K, Iwakuma M. "A Buddhist-Based Meditation Practice for Care and Healing: An Introduction and its Application." *International Journal of Nursing* 2013; 19 (Suppl. 2): 15-23.

5. The illustration on this page is an homage to the work of the Mexican cartoonist and artist Jose Guadalupe Posada (1852-1913). Much of his work is associated with the Central and South American holiday *Dia de los Muertos*, the Day of the Dead.

A relevant TEDx talk by Jim Nikas is at: http://www.youtube.com/watch?v=Hj1VNGHMNpA

Writing about the Day of the Dead in "The Labyrinth of Solitude," Octavio Paz, 1990 Nobel Prize winner for literature, states that, "Death defines life; a death depicts a life in immutable forms; we do not change except to disappear. Our deaths illuminate our lives. If our deaths lack meaning, our lives also lacked it."

About our modern view of death, Paz continues, "Everything in the modern world functions as if death did not exist. Nobody takes it into account, it is suppressed everywhere: in political pronouncements, commercial advertising, public morality and popular customs; in the promise of cut-rate health and happiness offered to all of us by hospitals, drugstores and playing fields. But death enters into everything we undertake, and it is no longer a transition but a great gaping mouth that nothing can satisfy. The century of health, hygiene and contraceptives, miracle drugs and synthetic foods, is also the century of the concentration camp and the police state, Hiroshima and the murder story. Nobody thinks about death, about his own death, as Rilke asked us to do, because nobody lives a personal life."

- Paz O. *The Labyrinth of Solitude*. New York: Grove Press, 1961.

6. Nick is right to bring up the role of health behaviors in preventing disease. Estimates from a number of studies estimate that 50% of U.S. deaths are attributable to lifestyle factors. Two comprehensive studies of this epidemiological research include:

- Molded AH, Marks JS, Stroup DF, Gerberding JL. "Actual Causes of Death in the United States 2000." *Journal of the American Medical Association* 2004; 291(10):1238-1245.

- Keeney RL. "Personal Decisions are the Leading Cause of Death." *Operations Research* 2008; 56(6): 1335-1347.

Nick is wrong, however, when he suggests that you can't change your genes. As Dr. Dean Ornish states: "Changing lifestyle actually changes your genes — turning on genes that keep you healthy and turning off genes that promote heart disease, prostate cancer, breast cancer, and diabetes — hundreds of genes in just three months." We'll hear much more from Dean Ornish in Lesson 6.

- Ornish D. "A Radical Alternative for Democrats and Republicans." *The Huffington Post*. August 29, 2012.

- Ornish D, Magbanua MJ, Weidner G, Weinberg V, Kemp C, Green C, Mattie MD, Marlin R, Simko J, Shinohara K, Hagg CM, Carroll PR. "Changes in Prostate Gene Expression in Men Undergoing an Intensive Nutrition and Lifestyle Intervention." *Proceedings of the National Academy of Sciences of the United States of America* 2008; 105(24): 8369-8374.

Despite roughly half of disease and death being caused by behavioral and social factors (it's been observed that your zip code is a better predictor of health than your genetic code!), these factors haven't received much attention in the "health" fields. Divisions of the National Institutes of Health are typically directed by laboratory scientists and physicians with little or no training in the behavioral and social sciences. I believe that the lack of exposure to these sciences is a primary reason why only a small fraction of research funding is devoted to behavioral and social sciences research. It's often difficult to support what you don't understand.

Lesson 2: Defensiveness

1. A riveting, if somewhat disgusting, description the 19th century frog boiling experiments may be found in:

There's long-standing debate over whether this frogboiling concept is actually true. In 19th century experiments, a frog was found to stay in the water only if the water very gradually heated. Or if its brain is removed.

- Sedgwick WT. "On Variations of Reflex-Excitability in the Frog, Induced by Changes Temperature." In N. Martin (ed.), *Studies From the Biological Laboratory*. Baltimore: N. Murray, Johns Hopkins University, 1888.

2. The frog exhibits standard defensive reactions, including: questioning the source ("Are you an expert on boiling water?"), *denial* ("This water isn't so hot"), and *downward social comparison* ("There are other frogs in worse condition than me"). Two excellent studies and a book examining defensive behavior are:

    *   Liberman L, Chaiken S. "Defensive Processing of Personally Relevant Health Messages." *Personality and Social Psychology Bulletin* 1992; 18(6): 669-679.

    *   Leffingwell TR, Neumann C, Leedy MJ, Babitzke AC. "Defensively Biased Responding to Risk Information Among Alcohol-Using College Students." Addictive Behaviors 2007; 32:158-165.

    *   Baumeister RF. *Escaping the Self: Alcoholism, Spirituality, Masochism, and Other Flights from the Burden of Selfhood*. Basic Books, 1991.

3. In academic and public health circles, there's a decades-old debate about using fear arousal to change behavior. Early research found an "inverted U-shaped curve" relationship between degree of fear arousal and attitude change. In other words, both low or no fear arousal and very high fear arousal produced little change in attitudes, whereas a moderate amount of fear produced a bigger change. More recent research finds that fear arousal changes behavior primarily when people are confident in their ability to change (what is called "self-efficacy").

    I think fear messages are like dirty bombs: they can influence change, but they're not specific. Fear messages can scare people who are at low risk, but are ignored by people who are at high risk. I also believe that these messages are often the refuge of the incompetent communicator, like a parent who resorts to yelling at or striking their children. Clever, well-constructed messages can engage intrinsic motives without resorting to fear.

4. By "ego" I mean the mechanism that maintains our perception of who we are. The ego can prevent us from seeing clearly who we are — from facing the truth about our selves. The philosopher Erkart Tolle calls this version of ego "the devil."

5. In "The Curse of the Self," psychologist Mark Leary states, "According to many spiritual traditions, the goal for the religious practitioner is to distinguish these desires of the personal ego-self from those of the 'true self,' which many religions conceive as an aspect or manifestation of the One (God, Allah, Tao, Brahman, or Great Spirit). Most spiritual traditions suggest that people are much more than the small, earthbound, psychological self that they imagine themselves to be and heed the True

Self rather than the personal ego."

- Leary MR. *The Curse of the Self: Self-Awareness, Egotism, and the Quality of Human Life*. Oxford: Oxford University Press, 2004.

6. Studies of ego and defensive behavior include:

- Nussbaum AD, Dweck CS. "Defensiveness Versus Remediation: Self-Theories and Modes of Self-Esteem Maintenance." *Personality and Social Psychology Bulletin* 2008; 34(5):599-612.

- Lambird KH, Mann T. "When do Ego Threats Lead to Self-Regulation Failure? Negative Consequences of Defensive High Self-Esteem." *Personality and Social Psychology Bulletin* 2006; 32(9): 1177-1187.

A careful review of the literature on exposure to information guided by defensiveness is:

- Hart W, Albarracin D, Eagly AH, Brechan I, Lindberg MJ, Merrill L. "Feeling Validated Versus Being Correct: A Meta-Analysis of Selective Exposure to Information." *Psychological Bulletin* 2009; 135(4):555-588.

7. The Greek stoic philosopher Epictetus (55-135 AD) said that if a man "opposes evident truths, it is not easy to find arguments by which we shall make him change his opinion. But this does not arise either from the man's strength or the teacher's weakness; for when the man, though he has been confuted [proven wrong] … is hardened like a stone, how shall we then be able to deal with him by argument?"

- Epictetus. *Discourses and Selected Writings*. New York: Penguin Classics, 2008.

In his commencement address to the 2005 graduating class of Kenyon College, the late, great David Foster Wallace indirectly referred to the ego as his natural default setting: "It's the automatic, unconscious way that I experience the boring, frustrating, crowded parts of adult life when I'm operating on the automatic, unconscious belief that I am the center of the world and that my immediate needs and feelings are what should determine the world's priorities … the so-called 'real world' will not discourage you from operating on your default settings, because the so-called 'real world' of men and money and power hums along quite nicely on the fuel of fear and contempt and frustration and craving and the worship of self. Our own present culture has harnessed these forces in ways that have yielded extraordinary wealth and comfort and personal freedom. The freedom to be lords of our tiny skull-sized kingdoms, alone at the center of all creation."

Wallace's "tiny skull-sized kingdoms" are his representation of ego.

- Wallace DF. *This is Water: Some Thoughts Delivered on a Significant Occasion, About Living a Compassionate Life*. New York: Little, Brown and Company, 2009.

A few decades ago our society received most of its information from a small number of media sources: primarily three channels of television providing a middle-of-the-road perspective. Today we have a vastly larger array of media sources and channels. We also have a far broader range of viewpoints that serve to protect our opinions from any outside challenge, resulting in ever-thicker defensive walls. Eli Pariser calls this effect the "filter bubble."

- Pariser E. *The Filter Bubble*. London: Penguin Books, 2011.

Much of my research over the past 20 years has focused on the impact of messages that are tailored to an individual's specific needs and interests. We've found that tailoring messages can significantly improve rates of health behavior change, and even influence a specific part of the brain related to long-term memories. However, as my wife Jeri uncharitably (but accurately) points out, tailoring also makes the ditch we've dug for ourselves even deeper.

8. The idea of ego "breaking open" is fundamental to many approaches to change. Twelve-step models of change (for example, Alcoholics Anonymous) emphasize the concept of "hitting bottom." It's also fundamental to epiphany experiences — the sudden or quantum changes in understanding and behavior.

An excellent book examining this process is:

- Miller WR and C'deBaca J. *Quantum Change: When Epiphanies and Sudden Insights Transform Ordinary Lives*. New York: Guilford Press, 2001.

9. Of all the books people recommended to me about grief and coping, Elizabeth Lesser's "Broken Open" really hit home. It was an inspiration for this book. Her gentle, thoughtful approach to finding growth in tragedy is a model for helping others.

- Lesser E. *Broken Open: How Difficult Times Can Help Us Grow*. New York: Random House, 2004.

10. Gabriel's question regarding tragic events (i.e., must we directly experience tragic events to see the truth clearly?) may have another answer as well: the transformational power of tragic art. In "The Birth of Tragedy," Friedrich Nietzsche writes that the arts "make life possible and worth living." More importantly, he points out that tragic art, rather

than depressing us, can be uplifting and transforming. In "Twilight of the Idols," Nietzsche writes, "The tragic artist is not a pessimist — it is precisely he who affirms all that is questionable and terrible in existence, he is Dionysian." A recent example is the movie "Melancholia," which deals with the end of the world. As *Los Angeles Times* film critic Betsy Sharkey puts it, "How does the world end? When it is in the hands of the cinematic master of human misery, dark Danish auteur Lars von Trier, as it is in 'Melancholia,' it ends in extraordinary, horrific, searing, aching and unthinkable ways. It is his most hopeful film yet."

For those interested in Nietzsche's work I would suggest a book by Richard Schacht, professor of philosophy at the University of Illinois:

• Schacht R. *Making Sense of Nietzsche: Reflections Timely and Untimely.* Chicago: University of Illinois Press, 1995.

Nietzsche's writing on loss of meaning in a modern world set the stage for 20th century existentialism, Viktor Frankl's Logotherapy ("Meaning Therapy"), and secular humanism.

Lesson 3: Self-Transcendence

1. In his 1918 book "The Sacred Beetle and Others," the French naturalist Jean-Henri Fabre observes in the Provençal countryside: "A nice, fresh patch of dung is not found just when you want it, in the barren plains overgrown with thyme; a windfall of this sort is as manna from the sky; only fortune's favorites receive so fair a portion. Wherefore the riches of today are prudently hoarded for the morrow."

Describing a particular dung beetle's journey rolling his ball of "manna" up a steep hill, Fabre's colorful prose approaches worship: "Perhaps it suits him to return to the heights. Against that I have nothing to say: the Scarab's judgment is better than mine as to the advisability of keeping to lofty regions; he can see farther than I can in these matters ... Now begins a Sisyphean labour. The ball, that enormous burden, is painfully hoisted, step by step, with infinite precautions, to a certain height, always backwards. We wonder by what miracle of statics a mass of that size can be kept upon the slope. Oh! An ill-advised movement frustrates all this toil: the ball rolls down, dragging the Beetle with it. Once more the heights are scaled and another fall is the sequel. The attempt is renewed, with greater skill this time at the difficult points: a wretched grass-root, the cause of the previous falls, is carefully got over. We are almost there; but steady now, steady! It is a dangerous ascent and the merest trifle may yet ruin everything. For see, a leg slips on a smooth bit of gravel! Down come ball and Beetle, all mixed up together. And the insect begins over again, with indefatigable obstinacy. Ten times, twenty times, he will attempt the hopeless ascent, until his persistence vanquishes all obstacles, or until, wisely recognizing the futility of his efforts, he adopts the level road."

This is a metaphor for purpose if ever I saw one!

- Fabre JH. (Translated by Alexander Teixeira de Mattos) *The Sacred Beetle and Others*. New York: Dodd, Mead & Co., 1918.

2. A detailed and modern description of dung beetle behavior may be found in:

- Simmons LW, Ridsdill-Smith (ed). *Ecology and Evolution of Dung Beetles*. Wiley, 2011.

Many thanks to the lead author, Professor Leigh Simmons at the Center for Evolutionary Biology, The University of Western Australia, for his personal communication, advice and descriptions of dung beetle behavior.

3. References to Khepri, the scarab god, include:

- Wilkinson RH. *The Complete Gods and Goddesses of Ancient Egypt*. New York: Thames & Hudson, 2003.

A comprehensive reference to ancient Egyptian history is:

- Shaw H. *The Oxford History of Ancient Egypt*. Oxford: Oxford University Press, 2000.

The Egyptian Book of the Dead begins with a prayer to Khepri:

"Hail to you, you having come as Khepri, even Khepri who is created of the gods. You rise and shine on the back of your mother (the sky), having appeared in glory as King of the gods."

This book is filled with gorgeous illustrations and hieroglyphics: an early graphic novel!

The Egyptian Book of the Dead. San Francisco: Chronicle Books, 1994.

4. This finding comes from studies using Self-Affirmation Theory.

- Steele C. "The Psychology of Self-Affirmation: Sustaining

the Integrity of the Self." In L. Berkowitz (Ed), *Advances in Experimental Social Psychology*. San Diego, CA: Academic Press, 1985.

5.   The study cited is:

   •   Crocker J, Niiya Y, Mischkowski D. "Why Does Writing About Important Values Reduce Defensiveness? Self-Affirmation and the Role of Positive, Other-Directed Feelings." *Psychological Science* 2008; 19:740-747.

6.   Discussion and conceptual organization of the transcendence concept can be found in the voluminous work of Professors Christopher Peterson and Martin Seligman. Lasting thanks to Professor Peterson for our discussions on this and other positive psychology subjects. He unfortunately passed away three weeks before I wrote these words. Pura Vida, Chris!

   •   Peterson C, Seligman MEP. *Character Strengths and Virtues: A Handbook and Classification*. Oxford: Oxford University Press, 2004.

7.   The study of self-transcendence took me to Aldous Huxley, Abraham Maslow and others who wrote philosophically about the concept. Aldous Huxley (1894-1963), author of "Brave New World" among many other novels, was a follower of the Indian Vedanta philosophy and one of the early "psychonauts" of the 20th century.

Aldous Huxley (1894-1963), author of Brave New World among many other novels, was also a follower of the Indian Vedanta philosophy.

While he apparently didn't believe that most people would achieve lasting self-transcendence through drugs, he was intrigued by them, first taking peyote in 1930 and LSD in 1955. On his deathbed, Mr. Huxley's wife reported giving him an injection of LSD: his dying wish.

Greater elaboration of his views on "downward transcendence" can be found in:

   •   Huxley A. *The Devils of Loudun*. Harper and Brothers, New York, 1953.

More about psychonautics in:

   •   Moro L, Simon K, Bard I, Racz J. "Voice of the Psychonauts: Coping, Life Purpose, and Spirituality in Psychedelic Drug Users." *Journal of Psychoactive Drugs* 2011; 43(3):188-198.

8. Huxley was a tremendous fan of classical music and the two were close friends for nearly two decades. Stravinsky's last orchestral composition was "Variations: Aldous Huxley in Memoriam."

9. Maslow's late-career observations about transcendent individuals are well worth reading. Both Huxley and Maslow had the opportunity to get to know many of the geniuses of their time: Einstein, Stravinsky, Schweitzer, and others. Both keen observers, they naturally looked for special qualities in special people. Transcendence was a consistent characteristic that they found.

   • Maslow AH. *The Farther Reaches of Human Nature*. New York: Penguin Books, 1976.

10. Maslow goes on to say: "Perhaps this is a price these people have to pay for their direct seeing of the beauty of world, the saintly possibilities in human nature, of the non-necessity of so much of human evil, or the seemingly obvious necessities for a good world; e.g., a world government, synergic social institutions, education in human goodness rather than for higher I.Q.'s or greater expertness at some atomistic job, etc. Any transcender could sit down and in minutes write a recipe for peace, brotherhood and happiness, a recipe absolutely within the bounds of practicality, absolute-attainable. And yet he sees this not being done; or where it is being done, then so slowly that the holocausts may come first. No wonder he is sad or angry or impatient at the same time that he is also 'optimistic' in the long run."

Lesson 4: Purpose

1. Having a purpose in life may be particularly relevant as we get older. To expand the quote at the beginning of this chapter, existentialist philosopher Simone de Beauvoir summarized the need for purpose as one makes this transition:

   "The greatest good fortune, even greater than health, for the old person is to have his world still inhabited by projects: then busy and useful, he escapes both from boredom and from decay ... There is only one solution if old age is not to be an absurd parody of our former life, and that is to go on pursuing ends that give our existence a meaning — devotion to individuals, to groups or to causes, social, political, intellectual or creative work. In spite of the moralists' opinion to the contrary, in old age we should wish still to have passions strong enough to prevent us turning in upon ourselves."

- Simone de Beauvoir, *The Coming of Age*. New York: Norton & Company, 1996.

2. The expanding behavioral and epidemiological science of purpose in life has indeed supported Winston's proposition. Relevant articles cited in the book include:

- Martin RA, MacKinnon S, Johnson J, Rohsenow DJ. "Purpose in Life Predicts Treatment Outcome Among Adult Cocaine Abusers in Treatment." *Journal of Substance Abuse Treatment* 2011; 40:183-188.

- Prairie BA, Scheier MF, Matthews KA, Chang CCH, Hess R. "A Higher Sense of Purpose in Life is Associated with Sexual Enjoyment in Midlife Women." *Menopause* 2011; 18(8):839-844.

- Kim ES, Sun JK, Park N, Kubzansky LD, Peterson C. "Purpose in Life and Reduced Risk of Myocardial Infarction Among Older U.S. Adults with Coronary Heart Disease: A Two-Year Follow-Up." *Journal of Behavioral Medicine* 2013; 36(2):124-133.

3. Two particularly relevant articles include:

- Boyle PA, Buchman AS, Barnes LL, Bennett DA. "Effect of a Purpose in Life on Risk of Incident Alzheimer Disease and Mild Cognitive Impairment in Community-Dwelling Older Persons." *Archives of General Psychiatry* 2010; 67(3):304-310.

- Boyle PA, Buchman AS, Wilson RS, Yu L, Schneider JA, Bennet DA. "Effect of Purpose in Life on the Relation Between Alzheimer Disease Pathologic Changes on Cognitive Function in Advanced Age." *Archives of General Psychiatry* 2012; 69(5):499-506.

Not only did Boyle and colleagues find that people with a strong purpose in life were 2.4 times less likely to get Alzheimer's Disease later in life, but they also observed specific pathologic changes in cognitive function. Imagine a drug that reduced your risk of Alzheimer's Disease by this amount. What would that drug be worth? This, in my opinion, goes back to the first chapter of the book, which asks "Who defines health?" If the National Institutes of Health and the medical profession as a whole pay little attention to these behavioral and social factors, we're the ones who pay the price.

4. Using a large longitudinal survey of the elderly, Professor Neal Krause, a colleague of mine at the University of Michigan, looked at the impact

on mortality of various components of meaning of life. Interestingly, he found that the "purpose" component had the most influence on mortality. In the abstract of his article, he states: "If the results from this study can be replicated, then interventions should be designed to help older people find a greater sense of purpose in life."

- Krause N. "Meaning in Life and Mortaliy." *Journal of Gerontology: Social Sciences* 2009; 64B(4): 517-527.

5. The recent evidence linking purpose to telomerase activity suggests that we may indeed be able to repair our own DNA — our genetic code. This research provides initial mechanistic evidence for the epidemiological associations presented in the book. The next question to answer is: Why does purpose in life repair your DNA?

- Jacobs TL, Epel ES, Lin J, Blackburn EH, Wolkowitz OM, Bridwell DA, Zanesco AP, Aichele SR, Sahdra BK, MacLean KA, King BG, Shaver POR, Rosenberg EL, Ferrer E, Wallace BA, Saron CD. "Intensive Meditation Training, Immune Cell Telomerase Activity, and Psychological Mediators." *Psychoneuroendocrinology* 2011; 36:664-681.

6. In his book 1897 book, "Suicide: A Study in Sociology," Emile Durkheim, the French father of sociology, writes that to remedy the then-increasing prevalence of suicide, "a man must feel himself more solidarity with a collective existence which precedes him in time, which survives him, and which encompasses him at all points. If this occurs, he will no longer find the only aim of his conduct in himself, and, **understanding that he is the instrument of a purpose greater than himself**, he will see that he is not without significance." He then asks "But what groups are best calculated constantly to re-impress on man this salutary sentiment of solidarity?

"**Not political** society …

"**Religious** society is equally **unadapted** to this function …

"Change have actually occurred in the constitution of the **family** which **no longer** allow it to have the same preservative influence as formerly ...

"Besides the society of faith, of family and of politics, there is one other of which no mention has yet been made; that of all workers of the same sort, in association, all who cooperate in the same function, that is, the **occupational group or corporation**." [my emphasis]

We still don't know whether an employer can create an environment that "constantly re-impresses" the kind of shared purpose suggested by Durkheim. (Wouldn't Charlie Chaplin have drawn endless comedic material from the modern corporation? The comic strip "Dilbert" is an example.) A positive expression of Durkheim's idea is presented in Chapter 6 with the highly successful Zingerman's Delicatessen, located in Ann Arbor, Michigan. This approach requires the rare leader possessing intelligence, courage, and moral fiber.

- Durkheim E. *Suicide: A Study in Sociology*. New York: The Free Press, 1951.

7. The study cited is:

- Niemiec CP, Ryan RM, Deci EL. "The Path Taken: Consequences of Attaining Intrinsic and Extrinsic Aspirations in Post-College Life." *Journal of Research in Personality* 2009; 73(3):291-306.

The conceptual foundation of this study is rooted in self-determination theory, developed by Richard Ryan and Edward Deci.

- Ryan RM and Deci EL. "Self-Determination Theory and the Facilitation of Intrinsic Motivation, Social Development, and Well-Being." *American Psychologist* 2000; 55(1):68-78.

8. From the Roman Stoic philosopher Seneca (4 BC - 65 AD), in his letter of consolation and advice to his friend Marcia, still debilitated by grief three years after the death of her teenaged son.

- Seneca. *Dialogues and Essays*. Oxford: Oxford University Press, 2007.

Lesson 5: Death

1. From "On the Nature of Things," by Lucretius (1st century BC).

- Lucretius. *On the Nature of Things*. London: Penguin Classics, 2007.

This 2,000-year-old poem of over 7,000 lines contains almost eerily modern thinking. Consider this section, which seems to presage atomic age physics. Fifteen hundred years later, the Catholic Church attempted to suppress writing about atomic particles, expressly forbidding the teachings of "atomism," and in fact burned people at the stake (for example, Bruno) for promoting such concepts.

"For what arises from the earth falls back to
        earth once more,
And that which was sent down to earth from heaven's
        aethereal shore
Is taken up again into the quarters of the sky.
Nor does Death demolish anything so utterly
That it annihilates the very atoms of its matter;
It only makes the combination of the atoms scatter.
From these it joins one particle with another — this is how
All things transform their shape and alter in
        their colour, now
Receiving sensation, and in an instant, yielding it up again.
That's how you know how much depends on
        the configuration
Of atoms, how they're held together, and in what position,
What motions they impart to one another or receive,
And that's the reason you should not mistakenly believe
Atoms permanently retain those qualities we see
Sliding across the surfaces of things suddenly
Coming into being and of a sudden passing away."

Lucretius's poem even suggests a type of reincarnation through the infinite connections and reconnections of matter:

"It's easy to believe that these same seeds of
        which we're made
In the here and now have in the past been
        frequently arrayed
In the same way, although we can't remember it because
A caesura has been cast between those different
        lives, a pause,
And the motions of their consciousness have
        wandered far astray."

Five hundred years after popes attempted to bury these ideas, the 20th century physicist Erwin Schrödinger expressed beliefs consistent with Lucretius's, only through the eyes of a preeminent scientist trained to see "the nature of things" through the mathematics of quantum mechanics:

"As surely as Mother Earth will engulf you tomorrow, so surely will she bring you forth anew to new striving and suffering. And not merely 'some day': now, today, every day she is bringing you forth, not once but thousands upon thousands of times, just as every day she engulfs you a thousand times over."

- Schrödinger E. *My View of the World*. Cambridge: Cambridge University Press, 1961.

An engaging book describing the ideas, loss, search, and suppression of Lucretius's poem *The Nature of Things* is:

- Greenblatt S. Swerve: *How the World Became Modern*. New York: Norton, 2011.

2. It's difficult to determine whether human beings are the only creatures on the planet who know they will die. In his book "The Bonobo and the Atheist," biologist Frans de Waal points out that many other animals grieve over their dead and states that he is "still not entirely convinced that we are the only ones with an inkling of our own death." (pg 210) He also, however, points out burial sites that include adornments for the afterlife go back as far as Cro-Magnon man — an indication of a belief in an existence beyond death that is not found among other species.

- de Waal F. *The Bonobo and the Atheist*. New York: Norton, 2013.

3. The Grim Reaper is, in general, correct. Take, for example, "Rabbit Hole," a movie with two popular actors, Nicole Kidman and Aaron Eckhart, about a couple whose son is killed in a car accident. The domestic total gross revenue of the movie has been, to date, a little more than $2 million. Compare this with the movie "Avatar", where the good guys pretty much come out fine. It grossed nearly 350 times as much.

In an interesting analysis, Ryan Niemiec and Stefan Schulenberg suggest " ... that movies, and in this case those that portray individuals who make adaptive choices in the face of death, may have a positive impact on those who watch them." In their article they quote Japanese filmmaker Akira Kurosawa's 1952 movie "Ikiru (To Live):" "I realize what they say about the nobility of misfortune is true. Because misfortune teaches us the truth. Your cancer has opened your eyes to your own life. We humans are so careless. We only realize how beautiful life is when we chance upon death."

- Niemiec RM and Schulenberg SE. "Understanding Death Attitudes: The Integration of Movies, Positive Psychology, and Meaning Management." *Death Studies* 2011; 35:387-407.

4. This argument was developed by the philosopher Todd May in:

- May T. *Death*. Montreal: McGill-Queen's University Press, 2009.

5. The premise of this discussion between the Dung Beetle and the Grim Reaper, that salience of death creates greater meaning in life, is affirmed in the following study:

- King LA, Hicks JA, Abdelkhalik J. "Death, Life, and Value: An Alternative Perspective on the Meaning of Death." *Psychological Science* 2009; 20(12): 1459-1462.

This well-established "scarcity of resources" argument of economics was also a favorite among the ancient Stoics. Epictetus, in his "Discourses," emphasizes the Stoic technique of considering the loss of a person or thing in order to strengthen the value of that person or thing. For example, Epictetus suggests that while kissing your child you say to yourself, "'Tomorrow you will die'; and to a friend also, 'Tomorrow you will go away or I shall, and never shall we see one another again ...'"

In "A Guide to the Good Life," a surprisingly peppy book about using Stoic philosophy in modern life, William Irvine, professor of philosophy, elaborates on this technique for parents: "To see how imagining the death of a child can make us appreciate her, consider two fathers. The first takes Epictetus's advice to heart and periodically reflects on his child's mortality. The second refuses to entertain such gloomy thoughts. He instead assumes that his child will outlive him and that she will always be around for him to enjoy. The first father will almost certainly be more attentive and loving than the second."

- Irvine WB. *A Guide to the Good Life: The Ancient Art of Stoic Joy.* New York: Oxford University Press, 2009.

6. From:

   - Nietzsche F. *The Gay Science.* New York: Vintage, 1974.

7. From:

   - Frankl VE. *Man's Search for Meaning.* Boston: Beacon Press, 2006.

8. Nietzsche here is referring to the distorted perspective of philosophic beliefs regarding truth and goodness. The slang "frog perspective" refers to the narrow perspective of a small, ground-dwelling creature.

   - Nietzsche F. "On the Prejudices of Philosophers." *Beyond Good and Evil.* New York: Penguin Classics, 2003.

9. The connection between meaning and purpose in life and religion is, of course, nearly universal. The best-known modern book about purpose is Rick Warren's "The Purpose Driven Life," which states at the outset:

   "If you want to know why you were placed on this planet, you must begin with God. You were born by his purpose and for his purpose."

   Another strong voice on this side of the discussion is the philosopher William Lane Craig, who writes:

   "The point is this: if God does not exist, then life is objectively meaningless; but man cannot live consistently and happily knowing that life is meaningless; so in order to be happy he pretends life has meaning. But this is, of course, entirely inconsistent — for without God, man and the universe are without any real significance."

- Craig WL. "The Absurdity of Life Without God." *The Meaning of Life* (E.D. Klemke editor). Oxford: Oxford University Press, 2000.

10. Christopher Hitchens took a very different tack, stating that meaning in life could be self-determined, and in fact felt that it was critical to be free to self-determine meaning and purpose: "... What makes my life meaningful: struggling myself to be free and trying to help others to be free, too." Pure Nietzsche.

You can find the debate between Craig and Hitchens at:

http://www.youtube.com/watch?v=x9NlRKJBKt4

- *William Lane Craig and Christopher Hitchens on the Purpose of Human Existence.* April 4, 2009. Biola University.

William Lane Craig goes on to write that "... if God does not exist and there is no immortality, then all the evil acts of men go unpunished and all the sacrifices of good men go unrewarded. But who can live with such a view?" Craig seems to be suggesting that a requirement for coping with a chaotic, unfair world is a belief in God and a just afterlife.

This doesn't strike me as a valid rationale for believing in God. Or, as necessarily true. Intelligent individuals have found ways to cope with the world without requiring religion. In fact, many have had strong, self-transcending purposes, including Sinclair Lewis ("It is, I think, an error to believe that there is any need of religion to make life seem worth living."), Albert Einstein, Carl Sagan, Thomas Edison, Ayn Rand, George Bernard Shaw, Arthur C. Clarke, H.G. Wells, Ulysses S. Grant, Ludwig van Beethoven, Wolfgang Amadeus Mozart, Mark Twain, Frank Lloyd Wright, and Paul Newman, to name a few. Others may be found in:

- Barker D. The Good Atheist: *Living a Purpose-Filled Life Without God.* Berkeley CA: Ulysses Press, 2011.

11. Study referred to is:

- Bartal IBA, Decety J, Mason P. "Empathy and Pro-Social Behavior in Rats." *Science* 2011; 334:1427-1430.

12. Study referred to is:

- Warneken F, Tomasello M. "The Roots of Human Altruism." *British Journal of Psychology* 2009; 100:455-471.

This research includes an excellent elaboration on the source of altruistic behavior. As the authors conclude:

"Our claim is thus that the altruistic tendencies seen in early human ontogeny reflect a natural predisposition. Socialization can build upon this predisposition, but it is not its primary source. Human cultures cultivate rather than implant altruism in the human psyche."

13. Special thanks to Dr. Laurent Lehmann from the University of Lausanne's Department of Ecology and Evolution and Dr. Michael Bonsall from Oxford University's Department of Zoology for their research in this area, and for their assistance with Winston's comment.

- Lehmann L and Keller L. "The Evolution of Cooperation and Altruism — a General Framework and a Classification of Models." *Journal of Evolutionary Biology* 2006;19(5):1365-1376.

- Bonsall MB and Wright AE. "Altruism and the Evolution of Resource Generalism and Specialism." *Ecology and Evolution* 2012;2(3):515-524.

An exceptional book on the subject is by Dr. Matt Ridley:

- Ridley M. *On the Origins of Virtue*. New York: Viking Press, 1996.

Toward the end of his book, Ridley writes, "Our minds have been built by selfish genes, but they have been built to be social, trustworthy and cooperative. That is the paradox this book has tried to explain."

14. Giving examples of altruistic behavior among dolphins, whales, elephants, chimpanzees and bonobos, Dr. Frans de Waal states that, "There is now increasing evidence that the brain is hardwired for social connection, and that the same empathy mechanism proposed to underlie human altruism may underlie the directed altruism of other animals."

- de Waal F. "Putting the Altruism Back Into Altruism: The Evolution of Empathy." *Annual Review of Psychology* 2008; 59:279-300.

Other research clearly demonstrates benefits, both psychological and physiological, of providing support to others.

- Brown SL, Nesse RM, Vinokur AD, Smith DM. "Providing Social Support May Be More Beneficial Than Receiving It: Results From a Prospective Study of Mortality." *Psychological Science* 2003; 14(4):320-327.

- Smith AM, Loving TJ, Crockett EE, Campbell L. "What's Closeness Got to Do With It? Men's and Women's Cortisol Responses When Providing and Receiving Support." *Psychosomatic Medicine* 2009; 71: 843-851.

The point here is that, contrary to William Lane Craig's conjecture that without God we will revert to barbarians, the science suggests otherwise: that transcendent core values and purpose are most likely hardwired into us through evolutionary selection, and it is up to society to cultivate or destroy this wiring.

I'm not claiming here that God does or does not exist. I've witnessed events that appeared miraculous. However, I believe that I simply lack the physical instrumentation to know whether God exists. In this book, I'm suggesting that one does not require God to have meaning and purpose in life or, for that matter, to be good.

15. From Steve Jobs' 2005 commencement speech at Stanford University.

The extended version of this statement is: "Death is very likely the single best invention of Life. It is Life's change agent. It clears out the old to make way for the new. Right now the new is you, but someday not too long from now, you will gradually become the old and be cleared away."

Jobs must have read 2,000-year-old Lucretius:

"Thus the sum of things is every hour renewed, and thus, in order to thrive, all mortal creatures need each other. While some are ascendant, some recede, and generations are renewed again in a brief space, passing life's torch, like relay runners in a race."

Lesson 6: Change

1. Books describing impressive life purposes include:

- Durant W. *On the Meaning of Life*. Frisco, TX: Promethean Press, 2005.

- Friend D. *The Meaning of Life: Reflections in Words and Pictures on Why We Are Here*. New York: Little Brown & Co,1991.

- Loehr J. *The Power of Story*. Free Press. New York: Free Press, 2008.

- Covey SK. *7 Habits of Highly Effective Families*. New York: St. Martin's Griffin, 1997.

2. In their book "Quantum Change," William Miller and Janet C'de Baca found that rapid shifts in core values coincided with sudden positive

change in behavior. This rapid or "quantum change" process isn't part of most models and theories of behavior change.

- Miller WR and C'de Baca J. *Quantum Change: When Epiphanies and Sudden Insights Transform Ordinary Lives*. New York: Guilford Press, 2001.

The focus on core intrinsic values and discrepancy between one's values and how one's life is actually lived is emphasized in an approach to behavior change called Motivational Interviewing.

- Miller WR and Rollnick S. *Motivational Interviewing: Preparing People for Change*. New York: Guilford Press, 2002.

3. Zingerman's Deli, Roadhouse, Bakehouse, and other businesses are among the most successful and beloved in Ann Arbor, Michigan. Now with a strong national following, Zingerman's has been named "the coolest small company in America" by *INC. Magazine*. Co-founder Ari Weinzweig's book about building a great business focuses attention on a grass-roots approach to creating a company mission. Mario Batali called the book a "magnificent tome" that "will help anyone interest to learn how to do the right thing (and increase sales) without selling out to the man."

- Weinzweig A. *A Lapsed Anarchist's Approach to Building a Great Business*. Ann Arbor: Zingerman's Press, 2010.

Many thanks to Ari, Peter Sickman-Garner, and Ryan Stiner for arranging and illustrating the Zingerman's mission, logo, and food for this panel, and to Ari for all the great meals!

4. Three of many relevant books by Dr. Dean Ornish, founder and president of the Preventive Medicine Research Institute, include:

- Ornish D. *Eat More, Weigh Less*. New York: HarperCollins, 1993.

- Ornish D. *Love & Survival: 8 Pathways to Intimacy and Health*. New York: HarperCollins, 1998.

- Ornish D. *The Spectrum: A Scientifically Proven Program to Feel Better, Live Longer, Lose Weight, and Gain Health*. New York: Ballantine Books, 2007.

Lesson 7: Life or Death?

1. Particular lifestyles behaviors can create the foundation for more vitality and willpower. Behaviors that are consistently related to vitality and willpower include sleep, presence or mindfulness, physical activity, creativity, and an appropriate diet. One could argue that other behaviors, for example, substance abuse behaviors (cigarette smoking, excessive alcohol consumption, drug abuse) could reduce our energy and should be included in this list. I think that a good starting point, however, would be Sleep, Presence, Activity, Creativity, and Eating well. In other words, giving yourself **S.P.A.C.E.**

    SLEEP is an often-ignored aspect of our health and well-being; chances are you could use more of it. A more detailed clinical discussion of sleep management may be found at:

    *   Schutte-Rodin S, Broch L, Buysse D, Dorsey C, Sateia M. Clinical guideline for the evaluation and management of chronic insomnia in adults. *Journal of Clinical Sleep Medicine* 2008; 4(5):487-504.

    An excellent lay publication for better sleep is:

    *   Epstein LJ and Mardon S. *The Harvard Medical School Guide to a Good Night's Sleep*. New York: McGraw-Hill, 2007.

    There are also a number of new, increasingly non-invasive devices that measure sleep.

    PRESENCE or mindfulness is another area that does not receive much attention from the medical establishment. Yet there is overwhelming data supporting meditation and associated instruction for vitality and general well-being, and for the management of pain, anxiety, depression. Jon Kabat-Zinn, founder of the Center for Mindfulness in Medicine, Health Care, and Society at the University of Massachusetts, defines mindfulness as *"awareness, cultivated by paying attention in a sustained and particular way: on purpose, in the present moment, and non-judgmentally. It is one of many forms of meditation, if you think of meditation as any way in which we engage in (1) systematically regulating our attention and energy (2) thereby influencing and possibly transforming the quality of our experience (3) in the service of realizing the full range of our humanity and of (4) our relationships to others and the world."*

    *   Kabat-Zinn J. *Mindfulness for Beginners: Reclaiming the Present Moment in your Life*. Boulder, Colo: Sounds True, 2012.

    As stated in Lesson 4 (Purpose), individuals undergoing meditation instruction are more likely to develop a purpose, which in turn, increases the repair of your DNA.

In a recent study, Dr. Christopher Niemiec and his colleagues found that, when considering their own mortality, individuals who are more mindful increased their endorsement of self-*transcendent* values whereas individuals who were less mindful increased their endorsement of self-*enhancing* values.

Niemiec CP, Brown KW, Kashdan TB, Cozzolino PJ, Breen WE, Levensque-Bristol C, Ryan RM. Being present in the face of existential threat: The role of trait mindfulness in reducing defensive responses to mortality salience. *Journal of Personality and Social Psychology* 2010; 99(2):344-365.

ACTIVITY doesn't have to mean hours of exertion and sweating. One can readily work more activity into a daily lifestyle. An excellent starting point for physical activities that create more vitality may be found at:

*   Department of Health and Human Services. *Be Active Your Way: A Guide for Adults*. ODPHP Publication No. U0037. October, 2008.

CREATIVITY is the least researched area of the S.P.A.C.E. behaviors, though qualitative reports of the beneficial effects of creativity, particularly art therapy for patients, have been cited for decades. More recently, studies using quantitative science and rigorous research designs have demonstrated clear benefits of creative activities on energy, well-being, and even longevity. For reasons I do not fully understand, much of this work has been conducted in Sweden.

*   Wikstrom BM, Theorell T, Sandstrom S. Medical health and emotional effects of art stimulation in old age. A controlled intervention study concerning the effects of visual stimulation provided in the form of pictures. *Psychotherapy and Psychsomatics* 1993; 60(3-4):195-206.

*   Konlaan BB, Bygren LO, chanson SE. Visiting the cinema, concerts, museums or art exhibits as determinant of survival: A Swedish fourteen-year cohort follow-up. *Scandinavian Journal of Public Health* 2000; 28(3):174-178.

*   Bygren LO, Konlaan BB, Johansson SE. Attendance at cultural events, reading books or periodicals, and making music ro singing in a choir as determinants for survival: Swedish interview survey of living conditions. *British Medical Journal* 1996; 313(7072):1577-1580.

*   Masutani T, Yamamoto Y, Konishi J, Maeda K. Effects of music and art education in early life and oral functions on the QOL of the

Takarazuka Revue Company OG compared with general elderly females. *Psychogeriatrics* 2010; 10:4-14.

- Burt EL, Atkinson J. The relationship between quilting and well-being. *Journal of Public Health* 2011; 34(1):54-59.

EATING WELL has a clear impact on vitality. While there will likely always be controversy over what and how much to eat, there are aspects of diet on which most experts agree. The Mediterranean diet has been carefully studied for decades and demonstrates long-term improvements in energy, weight control, and reduced likelihood of disease. It's also relatively easy to adopt. Dr. James Hill, Professor and Director of the Center for Human Nutrition at the University of Colorado notes that different diets may influence people differently and that our genes may predispose our response to variations in diets. This suggests that you might want to try different diet approaches: a Mediterranean diet, a glycemic index diet, a low-fat diet. There are commonalities in these diets but one may work better for you than for your friend.

For more information regarding glycemic indices and loads of specific foods see:

- Foster-Powell K, Holt SHA, Brand-Miller JC. International table of glycemic index and glycemic load values: 2002. *American Journal of Clinical Nutrition* 2002; 76:5-56.

For an excellent study of the effects of the Mediterranean diet and physical activity see:

- Landaeta-Diaz L, Fernandez JM, Silva-Grigoletto MD, Rosado-Alvarez D, Gomez-Garduno A, Gomez-Delgado F, Lopez-Miranda J, Perez-Jimenez F, Fuentes-Jimenez F. Mediterranean diet, moderate-to-high intensity training, and health-related quality of life in adults with metabolic syndrome. *European Journal of Preventive Cardiology* 2013; 20(4):555-564.

There are many others, but three books discussing diet by experts in the field include:

- Ornish D. *The Spectrum: A Scientifically Proven Program to Feel Better, Live Longer, Lose Weight, and Gain Health*. New York: Ballantine Books, 2007.

- Kessler D. *The End of Overeating*. New York: Rodale, 2009.

- Willett WC and Skerrett PJ. *Eat, Drink, and Be Healthy: The Harvard Medical School Guide to Healthy Eating*. New York: Free Press, 2001.

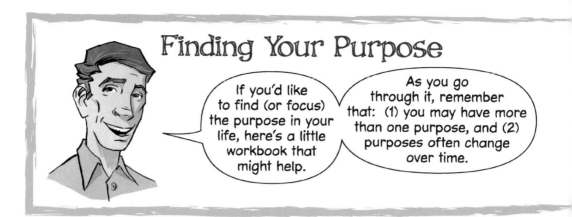

Finding Your Purpose

"If you'd like to find (or focus) the purpose in your life, here's a little workbook that might help.

"As you go through it, remember that: (1) you may have more than one purpose, and (2) purposes often change over time."

"Be ready for someone when they need me. Because I've had so much help and love from other people when I needed them!"

"To help the poor, the sick and the dying, and to help ignite in them a spiritual awareness. To serve God."

"To be a gentleman."

"To paint pictures that express the emotions of my breast cancer experience."

"To create a new business that helps people change their behaviors through finding purpose in their lives."

"To study and better understand nature, then give this knowledge to others. To be more engaged with my partner."

"To give the children in my school a clean building. To serve God."

Achievement   Independence   Security

Community   Kindness   Self-Control

Creativity   Relationships   Spirituality

Enjoyment   Reputation   Tradition

Expertise   Responsibility   Vitality

First, circle the 3-5 words or phrases that describe the core values that are the most important to you.

Why did you select these values?

What do you hope people will say at your memorial service?

_____

_____

_____

_____

_____

_____

_____

_____

_____

_____

_____

_____

_____

Now it's time to write your own purpose, based on the core values you chose earlier and the way you'd like to be remembered.

As you formulate your purpose, you may want to keep in mind what Rachel Remen said: "Often finding meaning is not about doing things differently; it is about seeing familiar things in new ways."

My Purpose

_____
_____
_____
_____
_____
_____
_____
_____
_____
_____
_____
_____
_____
_____
_____
_____
_____
_____
_____
_____
_____
_____
_____

You can go to our website, www.dungbeetlepress.org, to download an app that helps you monitor and study your own Life-Purpose Alignment.

My Life-Purpose Alignment

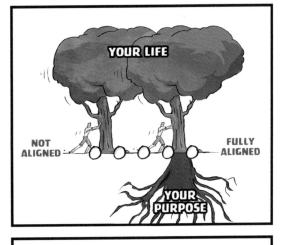

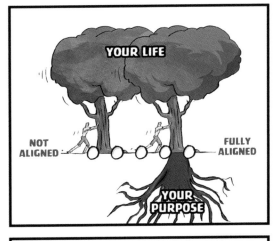

Author's Note and Acknowledgments

My friend Jeremy Nobel, Harvard physician and founder of the Foundation for Art & Healing, calls this book a "trauma narrative." Survivors of war, illness, and earthquakes have a story they *need* to tell. Whether as a book, poem, painting, dance, piece of music, or some other artistic expression, that story *has* to come out. Like a baby. Or a poison.

This is to say that writing *On Purpose* was therapeutic for me, an experience both beautiful and painful. Beyond therapy, however, my epiphany experience on Lake Michigan took me down a rabbit hole with no end in sight. I thank my wife Jeri for giving me the space to jump into this rabbit hole and, not looking back, come out the other end.

Much of the philosophy and science I encountered on this journey was new to me. I have many people to thank for helping me navigate, organize, and illuminate the path. Particularly, long discussions with Drs. Jim Loehr and Dean Ornish provided tremendous insight into purpose and meaning in life. Dean's assistance is portrayed in the book; Jim's program at the Human Performance Institute has had a major influence on my personal life, and is expressed throughout *On Purpose*.

University of Michigan professors Pedja Klasnja and David Baker, along with Benjamin Price, provided advice and direction related to many of the book's philosophical and religious aspects. *Benjamin, you will be missed.* Dr. David Abrams at the American Legacy Foundation provided scientific and personal insight into grief and loss.

As I started this project, I had no idea that one of my main characters would be a dung beetle (Winston). Professor Leigh Simmons at the Center for Evolutionary Biology, The University of Western Australia, was extremely helpful in reviewing my descriptions of dung beetle behavior. Every dung beetle researcher I encountered seemed to love his or her subjects. Of the organisms that effectively recycle excrement, dung beetles must be the most enjoyable to observe, and they easily beat hanging around with flies.

Drs. Laurent Lehmann from the University of Lausanne's Department of Ecology and Evolution, Michael Bonsall from Oxford University's Department of Zoology, and Jessica Purcell from the University of British Columbia's Department of Zoology reviewed and helped me refine Winston's comments regarding evolutionary models of cooperation and altruism.

Ohio State University professor Jennifer Crocker's research on self-affirmation, self-transcendence, and defensiveness was pivotal, and her personal communication is greatly appreciated. Dr. Kenneth Resnicow from the University of Michigan provided extremely useful comments and advice regarding the relationship between core values and purpose. Elizabeth Lesser's *Broken Open* was the most helpful book I read early during my process of grieving. It provided new insight, for me at least, into defensiveness and ego.

The decision to write a graphic novel emerged after months of wrestling with various formats. Finally my close friend, screenwriter Monte Montgomery, and I decided that a graphic novel might be a playful but powerful way to convey the personal story, the philosophy, and the science. Monte provided help through the entire course of this book, and without his expertise in storytelling it never would have been written.

Once the format was chosen, the next daunting step was identifying the creative talent to visually bring "On Purpose" to life. A conversation over a bottle of cabernet in New York City with David Erwin, Creative Director at DC Comics, provided eye-popping insight into the complexities of conveying the radically diverse emotional themes I was seeking.

Then I was lucky enough to find Kody Chamberlain, a Cajun from Lafayette, Louisiana. In one artist, Kody conveyed the emotions I was looking for, and then some. As laid back as I wasn't, Kody patiently breathed shadow and light, dark inks and soft pastels, and stark realism and magical thinking into the story. Sketching out ideas in Lafayette's coffee shops, listening to Zydeco, and eating boudin sausage with Kody were experiences that I'll always treasure.

I asked Kody for a "Zen master of lettering" (the bubbles of dialogue) and he recommended Kel Nuttall from North Pole, Alaska. (Yes, the comic and graphic novel industry takes you to far reaches!) From his underground lair, Kel created lettering for the book that demonstrates the art and skill of his craft.

Special thanks to Thomas Goetz, former Executive Editor at Wired Magazine, for providing encouragement and helping me to think about the audiences for *On Purpose*. Thanks also to David Owens for his help on the many logistic details of publishing and for his support. Many thanks to Lesa Huget for her careful and thoughtful copy editing.

Finally, sincere thanks to Jeri, Rachael, Josh, Mom, Dad, David Rossiter, Michael Huget, Julien Smith, Roger Magoulas, Michael Mosallam, Danielle Giuseffi, Leslie Stainton, Rory Crook, and Ryan Mark-Griffin for their thoughtful feedback on early drafts.

Vic Strecher
August, 2013